In ~~love~~ sync with poetry!

OrangeBooks Publication

Smriti Nagar, Bhilai, Chhattisgarh - 490020

Website: **www.orangebooks.in**

© Copyright, 2023, Author

All rights reserved. No part of this book may be reproduced, stored in a retrieval system, or transmitted, in any form by any means, electronic, mechanical, magnetic, optical, chemical, manual, photocopying, recording or otherwise, without the prior written consent of its writer.

In ~~love~~ Sync with poetry

Kevin R Gandhi

OrangeBooks Publication
www.orangebooks.in

Acknowledgement

Growing up, I did have an imaginary "Thank you" speech ready to gracefully receive a potential Bollywood award. I'll be honest; I never did imagine publishing a book full of poetries. Now that we're at it, my late mum is the first one that comes to my mind. Nothing that I am, would have been possible without you Maa! - THANK YOU!!!

I'd then like to thank the almighty for everything that exists in my life or doesn't. My dad, for always supporting almost every decision I take (minus my solo bike rides or my junk food choices).

My Naani (Maternal Granny), who is my ultimate coolest inspiration ever! The rest of my family, all elders in the clouds and the ones rocking it on land, my cousins and my smart little nephews and adorable nieces. I'd like to thank each one of you for always being there and teaching me the important lessons about life.

My friends, especially the ones that helped me on each step whilst the book was in the making and hence received a free copy and of course, the ones that have bought this book with an intention of reading it beyond this page. I'd like to thank everyone that I've crossed paths with and have shared a part of my life journey.

A special Thank you to all my teachers, bosses, mentors and colleagues. A double special mention about Mukesh Sir who helped me co-create my first ever prize-winning jingle back in school. That will remain my very first attempt and a step towards poetry.

Last but not the least (also coz she usually only reads the last few lines of all my long messages). I'd like to thank my muse for lending me a part of her life poetries that both inspired me and gave birth to the poet in me. She's known by quite a few names; I will forever remember her as "Poetry"

Thank you, "Poetry", I pray that you always remain "in style" In the Egypt of my heart, you'll always be my Nile.

Prologue

Once upon a time in an imagi-nation not very far away,
There lived a little girl, exceptionally brilliant
yet different from others in every way.
As she grew up, she discovered a few more voices
living inside her head,
Talking to them felt easy, conversing with the
deceiving world outside she started to dread.
She began weaving stories wrapped in meaningful rhymes;
Found herself lost in her own fairytales quite a lot of times.
One fine summer afternoon there was a tinkle on her phone,
He was technically a stranger but felt a lot like her own.
He on the other hand grew up as a timid kid also very shy,
Life however had taught him lessons very early,
He never let things he loved go away, without giving it a try.
He called her "Poetry" and adored
how she always remained "in style."
To be able to connect with her better,
he did what he hadn't for quite a while.
He started writing poetries again, replying to her
life stories from another continent, all at once.
Lost in her imaginary world, he created
an extension to it - poetry was his new trance.
The rest as they say is now history,
most of which we intend to keep a mystery (for now).

My reason for compiling most of our fictitious rhyming conversations into a book and building a poetic pyramid of sorts, was not just to preserve the timeless tomb of a story that could have been, but to also glorify the afterlife of it – "The Friend Zone"

I wanted to normalize the idea of being friend zoned, especially for the youth of today and tomorrow. I also wanted to share and connect with everyone who likes reading and/or writing poetries and fairytales.

I have divided the book into two parts; the first is a random collection of our poetic duet, the second is a semi-imaginary story line with some of my favorite assorted poetries. There isn't a particular flow or an overall bigger picture to this book coz sometimes in my opinion, life is meant to be lived in single chapters, one rhyme at a time and treasure the chaos, the mixed signals and the incomplete!

Of course, for those who know, will know a few events with better context and for the ones that don't, well use what I've used for a major portion of this book – Your imagination ☺

I hope this book is able to, in some way, bring meaning to your dreams, peace to your life and if nothing a smile on your face or at least occupy a little of an inch in your library's space. #GODBLESS

Index

The Muse And Her Poet 1

Destiny And The Spark 2

The Girl By The Sea 4

A Story Incomplete 6

What Makes You Smile? 7

What Can You Do For Love? 8

A Small List Of Flaws 10

The Stare That Stayed 12

A Masterpiece Called Life 13

The List Of Why's 14

Hot And Cold 16

Feel My Pain? 18

She Can 19

Your Heartbeats Are My Inner Voice 20

The Pearly White Line of Possibilities 22

If Love Is Your War – Go All In 24

The Pursuit Of Something New 26

The Golden Rose 27

She Said, He Said 28

I Am Very Simple She Said 30

The Almighty's Plan 31

The Leap Of Faith 32

Expectations 34

In The Soul of My Sky 36

Your Drizzle Is My Rain 37

The Way To Her Heart is Through Her Brain! 38

What Is Love She Asked 40

And What about Closures, Then? 41

What Is Your Deepest Desire She Asked 42

The Story Untold 43

The White Dream 44

The Phoenix 46

Some Words That Need To Be Spoken 48

The Missing Ice-Cream 50

The Warrior Disguised As A Princess 52

The Mythical Goal 54

The Permanent Ink 56

The Carousel Called Life 58

The Other Person 60

The Lemon Tree 61

A Heart Painted Blue 62

The Rolling Dice 64

The Phoenix – Redefined 66

Two Frozen Hearts 68

The World's Smallest Lighthouse 70

Never Say Goodbye... 72

The Forbidden Fruit... 73

The Heart And The Mind Still Don't Sync 75

Just Like That 77

The Dream Car 78

The Beast with a Human Heart 80

The Complicated Clues 82

Every City Has Its Own Love Story........................... 84

The Princess without Her Crown 86

Look Into My Eyes.. 89

The Swansong 91

Alice In Wonderland 93

A Story To Remember 95

A Vow Not Taken and A Wow Mistaken 97

Part II

Hey There Sunshine: 26th July 2020......................... 100

The Miracle Unicorn 102

The Mermaid - Defined: 22nd August 2020............... 104

The Mighty Waterfall... 105

The Child in Her:... 107

Our First Coffee Meet: 21st Nov............................... 108

The Little Blue Fish... 109

The Mermaid and The Lost Sailor 112

Wishes And Dreams 114

Different Worlds: 115

Stories on the Rocks 116

I Shall Send You A Sign 118

A Sunflower without its Sunshine 120

Set Me Free 121

When It Rained From the Ground 122

Legend Of The P'quals 124

Learn the Flow 125

A Boat from My Sunset to Your Sunrise 126

Matched By Destiny 128

Wrecks Can Be Beautiful Too 130

The Genie He Found In the Sea 131

Shades of Blue 133

Don't Miss the Train 134

Just Coincidences or True Signs? 136

Old V/S New 138

A Rhyme Incomplete 140

My Heart Beats In the Sea 141

Why Do I Still Dream About You? 142

The Lost Mermaid 144

Same Boat Different Journeys 146

I Often Wonder 147

Making Magic Happen 148
Watch Your Dreams Come True 149
Is Love Enough? 150
The Road Unknown 151
The Divine Light across the Sea 152
The City with Seven Islands 154
A Lot Like A Waterfall 155
A Cloudy Sky 156
A Sky Without Stars 158
Can't Stop Won't Stop 160
The Wise Sorcerer 162
You're My Lobster 164
Old MonK & coKe (15th May 2022) 165
Lakes with Our Names 168
Living inside A Snowglobe 170
Is It Ever A Goodbye? 172
My Sunrise V/S Your Sunset 174
A Destiny – Manifested! 175
Into Your Eyes 177
Away From Your Eyes 179

In ~~love~~ sync with poetry!

The Muse And Her Poet

She wrote:

Sometimes I just don't have the right poetry,
Sometimes I hope you'd write one for me,

Write me a poetry that fits with the picture please!

He replied:

Sometimes I just don't have the right poetry.
Sometimes I just hope you'd write one for me.

Saying this with an enchanting smile,
she stared in his eyes for a while.

Lost into her eyes, he found himself and surrendered!
"Not just one! My poetries will now begin
but never end" he murmured.

Time stood still, and so did that stare
and their heartbeats,
Thereafter, for every picture she gave him,
he wrote a poetry that fits!

Destiny And The Spark

<u>She wrote:</u>

There is a little bit of love in everything I do,
There is life beyond living –
there is so much more to you!

There are memorable moments, there are cuddles,
and there are smiles!
There is teaching; there is learning –
when we walk together for miles!

You are a little piece of me;
you are a treasure to my heart.
I knew it from the beginning,
from our very first spark.

He replied:

The spark was suppressed,
left stranded on an island.
In the middle of the sea in broad daylight
yet hidden like a diamond.

He wasn't ever doubtful of his own existence,
Neither did he ever lack the persistence.

And yet! Destiny had to turn her back towards the spark.
For reasons unknown forced to keep him in the dark.

Defeated, yet hopeful the spark
knew he had to keep faith.
Knowing that the lost returns
with the waves if truly yours,
sometimes, you just have to wait!

The Girl By The Sea

A)

You recede even faster than
you move close to the shore,
The sound of you that I've gotten used to,
I simply keep coming back for more.

It's been a low tide for some time now
and I can't complain.
Persistent I always was, patient too I shall surely remain.

I believe I shall see you soon if it's truly meant to be
I'll wait at the shore for the waves to come back to me!

B)

Have you ever ventured out alone into the sea?
Even though a scary decision
it could initially seem to be.

From the known safe roads
on to the subtly unknown sand.
As you move to deeper waters
with bands of hope on your hand.

The excited waves come forward
and welcome you within,
Chances of falling in love with
the new immediately, are thin!

But as you keep walking further
you clearly are able to see,
How exactly at this time and place
you were always meant to be!

How every other distraction
is out of mind and your sight,
How you're finally at peace, where you've always
belonged, between the day and night!

Kevin R Gandhi

A Story Incomplete

She Wrote:

You followed the trails of her dark mind;
she tried so hard to leave the mystery behind.

There is pain within and you failed to see,
she is tangled inside and wants to be free.

She carried with her – the hurt and the pain,
when you let her go it drove her insane.

The feeling so strong of what could have been,
A magical story that just went unseen.

It's a different kind of high – "The incomplete"
The reunion at another time that makes your heart beat!

He replied:

There are two incompletes
that are being tested with time,

One! On its final run,
the other holding on just to a rhyme.

One! Broken but not shattered,
the other almost half way yet scattered.

Only time will tell if history does repeat,
Or if the lost is destined to be complete!

In ~~love~~ sync with poetry!

What Makes You Smile?

She asked:

What makes you smile?

He replied:

What makes you smile?
I've been pondering on this question for a while.

And whilst I can list more than a thousand things,
and talk about the smile every memory brings.

I think I need to tell you
what makes me smile a bit more,
Coz that's what differentiates the surface from the core.

I smile a bit more every time I hear a chime;
I smile a bit more every time I read your rhyme.

I smile a bit more when I see the maple leaves,
Astonished at how someone so sincerely believes.

I smile a bit more when the feathers guarding my sleep let the sunlight through,
I smile a bit more when every morning, a sign on my tea cup reminds me that "Dreams do come true"

Kevin R Gandhi

What Can You Do For Love?

She asked:

What can you do for LOVE?

He replied:

Love beyond logic and live beyond boundaries,
now this may sound bookish,
but aren't most books inspired by real life stories?

The non-believers would still call them fairytales,
and that's exactly what they said
about dolphins and whales.

So the question here really shouldn't be,
"what can you do for love?"
Rather ask, "What wouldn't you do for true love?"

True love guards you from nightmares
and meets you in your dreams;
it could fetch the moon and the stars for you,
or just your favorite ice creams.

True love is like a turtle; it goes steady but grows slow.
It might not seem to fit you at first,
but well it surely does glow.

True love I guess can only be felt,
never something that one can explain.
If you're truly in love, go all out,
why should you even refrain?

A Small List Of Flaws

<u>She wrote:</u>

The broad forehead we may hate or the crooked teeth,
The frizzy hair so misplaced,
that never made you feel neat.

Flawed bodies we see, Flaws in planning life's trips!
Flawed decisions, we know, flaws in relationships!

I am not flawless; I will never claim to be!
I won't fake pride in my flaws,
nor do I feel it's a misery!

Yes, I have had a messy relationship front
Yes, I have been mean and Yes, I have been blunt.

So I may be judged, told that I am bad.
But that shouldn't break me, although, hell I'll feel sad!

He replied:

You think your flaws in comparison
to the perfect make you weak,
Whilst in reality they're the ones that keep you unique.

The broad forehead sits on those alluring eyes,
the crooked teeth surround one
of the most enthralling smiles.

With flawed relationships there's always
two sides to the coin,
the missing dots in life,
only by looking back you can join.

Call me crazy, but I still think it's necessary
to break a few laws,
and want to spend that forever with someone
who's fallen for those flaws.

The Stare That Stayed

He stared into her eyes and she couldn't look away.
Her heartbeats were on the rise,
yet! Somehow, she knew this was here to stay!

Their eyes spoke, their eyes listened.
As if they found something they were always seeking.

Still staring into her soul, he pulled her close.
Their heart beats aligned but everything
else around just froze.

As always, she just had that smile on her face,
Of wanting it all yet! Going at a slow pace.

Gathering some courage, he tried voicing his thoughts;
she shushed him instantly pausing the connecting knots.

Within a second, she saw him leaving
without a warning.
Startled suddenly she woke up early in the morning.

She opened her eyes again thinking he set off at dawn,
He lay right beside her, staring into his universe
 telling her that he can never be gone.

In ~~love~~ sync with poetry!

A Masterpiece Called Life

She asked:

What is your masterpiece?

He replied:

You can't connect the dots looking forward
you can only connect them looking back in time.
Trust that the dots will somehow connect to your future,
same way I've been leaving behind every rhyme.

Most unseen, unread and unliked,
I somehow still can't seem to cease
Looking back in time; I hope together,
we can call it "Our Masterpiece"

The List Of Why's

<u>She wrote:</u>

There are two souls in her body that makes her a mix.
It's almost a puzzle that is so hard to fix!

She would let you come close
and then cut off the strings.
You'll feel like the moment ends, even before it begins!

But if you stay longer, you'll start figuring out.
She'll open up to you, clearing doubt after doubt!

In ~~love~~ sync with poetry!

He replied:

Dressed in flawless white she stood in front of me,
staring into my clueless eyes.
So much to tell, but with a finger on her lip,
Often, leaving me wondering with a list of Why's!

Why is she such a big puzzle that is so hard to fix?
Probably coz she's a mysterious treasure box that
cannot be unlocked with a bunch of tricks.

Why would she let you close to her
and suddenly cut off the strings?
Probably coz she ain't ready yet,
she's still healing under her wings.

Staying longer isn't a choice anymore,
there's nowhere else that I can be,
Darkness always isn't due to the lack of light,
sometimes, you gotta open your eyes,
so the truth you can see

Hot And Cold

She wrote:

Her heart is ice, her body is fire!
Her love is pure, she is desire!

She is bright like the sun; she is playful and fun!
She is abstract personified, and she has only begun.

She is cold winter breeze; she can freeze you to death!
She is warm with her love; she has sensual breath.

She is deep like an ocean, and vast like a sea.
She can drive you so crazy – romantically!

In ~~love~~ sync with poetry!

He replied:

Legends about the fire and ice,
He had read time and again but they didn't suffice.

Stories about the sun and the moon,
had only begun, why did they end so soon?

The warmth of her time, he kept seeking in every rhyme.
Waiting it out endlessly still didn't feel like a crime.

The depths of the sea and the storms of the ocean,
He had lived every story, every bit of her emotion.

And calmly by the shore,
he kept asking for more,

with faith waiting for a tomorrow that would grant
him "a forever" for his persistent honest devotion.

Feel My Pain?

She wrote:

Meaningless promises, I'm not sure if I trust.
I've felt it evaporating in the air.
I've seen it burning down to dust.

Stay as far as you can, before the feeling gets insane.
It is dark inside here; I don't want you to feel the pain!

He replied:

Don't look away yet! Don't give up on me.
I ain't asking you to trust me yet!
Only asking you to just be!

Promises spoken are probably broken,
Promises that are shared
are often kept and are truly cared.

Far isn't an option anymore,
some are built for the insane.
The deepest connection it is said;
is the one that can heal the pain with pain!

In ~~love~~ sync with poetry!

She Can

She wrote:

She can play with your mind; she can drive you to think.
She can mirror your face, She can be serious – yet wink.

She can sway you with truth or lure you with lies.
She can be extremely transparent
or she can dress in disguise.

She can create a perception that she wants you to see.
She can be what you want or she can mesmerize thee!

He replied:

She plays with my mind constantly;
nothing else is left to think.
It feels like a dream even now,
when things changed within a blink.

The stories about her truth or lies,
Are as good as a myth as about her disguise.

And whilst she's surely capable of creating a perception,
it feels everything about her is a hallucination.

The real her has been walking tirelessly
under the scorching sun,
Searching for her own shadow along the tracks,
always on the run!

Your Heartbeats Are My Inner Voice

She wrote:

Thoughts of you just light me up;
you are the thudding of my heart.
There is a steep long road ahead of us,
but I am ready to make this start.

Come let us take this leap of faith,
why stay at the edge and contemplate?

At max this leap will make us fall,
but without risking it, we will never at all!

In ~~love~~ sync with poetry!

He replied:

A small little kid went up the hills,
Seeking adventure and some new thrills.

The view from the top left him speechless,
yet! A few words he spoke loudly, nevertheless!

"This is beautiful" he shouted,
"Beautiful! Beautiful" someone else then replied.
Shocked for a moment he ran
to his mother on the other side.

Clueless about who sat on
the other side of the mountains.
He didn't know what an echo was,
hence had all the questions.

"It's your inner voice" his mother told him,
wanting to keep things a bit interesting,
"It resonates the truth multiple times"
she said suggesting.

My heart kinda echoed with the words I read above
Amazed I was at the timing, the coincidence and how.

And therefore, I shared this little tale with you.
 To tell you that my "inner voice"
multiplyingly resonates with you!

The Pearly White Line of Possibilities

She wrote:

I want to trust again but the scars have not yet gone.
I want to be in love but I seem to turn it down!

I try to give it a shot but the hurdles never seem to go.
Then time you say is running –
well I prefer to take it slow.

He sprinkled colors in my life –
to present its beauty too.
I painted it so black –
for I can't move to something new.

He replied:

The scars on the walls of your heart I see,
with experience, I know it's not an easy place to be.

And I know how every path you'd take,
the hurdles seem to block.
And hence sometimes before you run again,
it's important to just walk.

Walk along to slow the running time down,
breathe freely, heal and get your smile back.
Everything else I promise you'll see,
falling back right on track.

Your choice of "so black" too, I can very well see,
But there's always an actual choice, specially!
When it's meant to be!

There's always a pearly white line
of possibilities beyond the horizon,
where your tomorrow can forever be!

If Love Is
Your War – Go All In

She wrote:

The battle of the mind, it is all around thee!
The terrain in their head, you can barely see!

War, of any kind they say is an art.
Holy Scriptures always taught me
to love the enemy from the start!

I wonder if you should then stick to your moral law.
Or should you rather look
for your enemies' weakness and his flaw?

What would hurt you more – to crush or to be crushed?
Would it then be fair in war to break somebody's trust?

Should you attack with your might or kill if you must?
If everything is fair in war,
should you bring them down to dust?

In ~~love~~ sync with poetry!

He replied:

The battle of the mind, it is all around thee!
Fighting your own demons, your first war it should be.

War! Of any kind of course, is an art!
And hence in this case, you have to play an equal part.

You have to defeat the wrong,
so the right within you can win,
Leave the old bruises behind,
so the new can finally begin.

Everything is fair in love and war they say,
And hence if you're at war for Love's sake with
yourself, bring everything down to dust, you just may!

Coz if you win, you'd win a forever for yourself,
And even if you lose,
who better to lose to – than yourself!

The Pursuit Of Something New

She wrote:

Roses are red, Violets are blue!
They say nothing is impossible,
so let's do something new!

Let's change roses to blue, and violets to red!
Let us recreate the world, and leave nothing to dread!

The sense of freedom, that love for your dreams!
The fire inside me, it constantly screams.

He replied:

Roses are red, Violets are blue!
They say nothing is impossible,
and I am counting on it too.

Let's change the roses to blue, and the violets to red.
Let us recreate some rhymes, and leave nothing to dread.

That sense of freedom, the same love for your dreams,
The pending number of coffees and the ice creams!

Violets are red now and roses are blue,
Remember! My Blue will always
just be BLE without U!

In ~~love~~ sync with poetry!

The Golden Rose

She wrote:

She smiles like sunshine; she blushes like a rose!
She plays with her words, telling story in prose!

Every day is a new story, every minute seems like fun!
She will dance away to glory,
wearing a sweatshirt in the sun!

She is the same person who you know
– yet so different every day.
Hold her hand if you must, for she can swiftly run away.

He replied:

Her words have vanished, her stories have disappeared.
Darkness all around, from the rose, I haven't heard.

Every day is the same, nothing otherwise is fun,
Wondering why she needs to always be on the run?

Nature however, has its own way of healing.
Sometimes, it's wise to wait it out rather than appealing.

And hence it's okay if sunshine has her reasons,
Coz patience can wait longer than all seasons.

Until again when she starts telling her stories in prose,
I believe that the sun will reveal the golden rose!

She Said, He Said

She wrote:

I said: Don't be afraid of who you are,
To me, you are a shining star!

I said: Don't be afraid to laugh out loud,
To me, you are fun, and I am really proud!

I said: Don't be afraid to be bold or shy,
To me, you are a soul , with whom I will laugh and cry!

I said: Don't be afraid of your darker side,
To me, you are special, you just got mystified.

I said: Don't be afraid if the road seems steep,
To me, this seems fun, let's take this giant leap!

He replied:

We tend to say a lot of things to ourselves,
They often end up like unread books
on our book shelves.

Only if we were able to listen to our inner voice so often,
We wouldn't really be taking
a lot of regrets to our coffin.

Better late than never they say,
If only an inner voice could speak to by night
and you could hear it by day.

So even if there's a tiny chance that you can take,
You should think about it on your next coffee break.

I Am Very Simple She Said

He replied:

Simple? Simple has never been so complicated before,
it's been a while that I've felt
a beat like this from the core.

Simple! Is speaking your heart out!
Not staying away from communication creating doubt.

Simple! Is keeping things slow if not in a rush,
Not bringing it to a halt being nervy of the shussssh!

And yes! Simple is surely walking
with heels in your hand,
or letting your hair loose from that wired hair band.

Simple is being prompt with those alluring smiles,
Whilst walking barefoot on the sun kissed tiles.

Simple it would be if I could ask something to thee,
Yet! Getting to know my answer before
the important question, is important to me.

In ~~love~~ sync with poetry!

The Almighty's Plan

This is a story about a fresh water fish born in the sea,
all her life she thought this was
where she was meant to be.

The goodness in her heart made her sacrifice,
Care for everyone to the extent of letting
her dreams hide in disguise.

She often had visions of streams, rivers and lakes.
Her natural habitat kept calling out to her, yet! A lot
of determination to face the truth it takes.

Along came a storm which uprooted
everything in the reef.
She felt her life had turned upside down
and there was only dark grief.

It was only as the storm passed that she realized,
she had landed in a stream far away
and she was truly surprised.

Surprised at the fact that she finally felt at peace,
Surprised that her internal wars
had finally come to cease.

The almighty's plan she was finally able to see,
Life happens to all, and always, as it's meant to be!

The Leap Of Faith

<u>**She wrote:**</u>

I'd like to spread my wings and fly,
I'd like to take a leap so high.

For just one more time I need to try,
When I know I am about to touch the sky.

Yet! I lay so quite now;
I keep staring at the sky above.

When I know it's time to take a leap.
I'm rock bottom where it feels so deep.

I need your hand to stretch out for me,
Even if I say just let me be!

He replied:

The leap of faith it's called for a reason.
A stretched hand giving comfort will count as treason.

The universe rewards the ones
who truly believe and are ready to try.
Giving up on everything they had ashore,
to spread their wings and fly.

And once you take off, you see
that it was all about the first step,
and how everything else was always
ready and well kept.

The inner voice you hear within every day,
Talks to you in spite of anything else you may say.

It truly is the voice of your destined dreams.
Don't doubt it! It's real and hence this way it seems.

Expectations

She wrote:

Know what you did to my expectations?
You build them up, and then let me down.
I didn't listen to my hearts hesitations!
Now the consequences are my thorny crown.

What was it that you had to suppress?
Were my hopes and ambition too much to handle?
Your love is supposed to brighten not depress.
For me, you couldn't even light a candle.

I didn't expect flowers moonlit nights and crazy wooing.
But killing me was what you eventually came to doing.

Yes it is hard, but there's nothing to discuss.
Let me make it clear, there's no more 'us'.

He replied:

Expectations and disappointments are like yin and yang.
A true prayer of love however, works like a boomerang.

The farther you toss the idea of love away,
faster it comes back to you to stay.

It isn't your fault when the
real most random things seem fake,
Even though with patience for each day,
every night it stays awake.

Don't give up on your expectations, when the time
is right, they'll be somebody else's dreams.
For now enjoy the sunsets by the beach,
the coffees and the colorful ice creams.

In The Soul of My Sky

When everything was dark, I could see the stars.
They did seem to heal for a while,
but I never really forgot the scars.

It was a dark clear night;
Hence the stars were shinning bright.

As time passed, back came the clouds,
and so did all the doubts.

The twinkling stars I could no longer see,
and just like in the past, I thought the light
had abandoned me.

Yet! Love and hope this time seemed to have
caught up with me,
And even though through the clouds, them stars every
day, I could no longer see.
They kept shining bright in the soul of my sky
still being a part of my destiny!

In ~~love~~ sync with poetry!

Your Drizzle Is My Rain

She wrote:

I'm running away forever, for on my own I belong.
The idea of being with someone,
is something way too strong!

You took away those hours from me –
it really didn't suffice.
My body felt like fire, but my heart as cold as ice!

So let us walk back in that alley,
let's do this one time again.
The dark clouds, the light wind and the drizzle –
this time let's wait back until the rain!

He replied:

These tracks you stand on that run endlessly.
They run alone yet they run parallely.

And hence the idea of being with someone,
Should be felt from within, very naturally.

Enjoy the drizzle till it lasts,
coz it rains when it has to rain,
A seed of forever fallen into the soil of the soul
is destined to grow again.

The Way To Her Heart is Through Her Brain!

She wrote:

Can you see beyond the good looks?
Can you handle lightning that comes with the rain?
She won't fit any character in your books,
She burns and scars, leaving an indelible stain.

She may look like a model,
But don't be fooled by her pose.
She can drive you to the bottle.
In case you try to pick this rose.

But perseverance can be rewarding
if you can persist and survive the strain.
Pay attention to the statutory warning,
The way to heart is through her brain.

He replied:

I find her intelligent and exceptionally witty,
yet! She's the one who often calls me smarty!

Does that mean to her brain I do appeal?
Does that mean her heart also does feel?

I know in my books it'll be tough
finding a relatable character.
And hence, A book on her I am writing,
chapter after chapter.

The present chapter, I call "the silver lining"
Next in line is the new year, "a new beginning?"

What Is Love She Asked

He replied:

Love is patient,
Love is persistent!

Love is sacrifice,
Love is compromise!

Love is this, Love is that!
Love is a dog, Love is a cat!

Love is old, Love is new!
Love stays forever with only a few.

Love is silly, Love is stupid!
Sometimes in denial about the cupid.

Love can only be felt but never explained.
It is about how much you gave yet never gained.

Love if pure will set you free,
And watch it happen again, when it's meant to be!

In ~~love~~ sync with poetry!

And What about Closures, Then?

He replied:

Closures are confusing, Closures are incomplete,
Sometimes they're like endless loops,
played on forward, rewind and repeat.

Closures need acceptance, Closures need might!
You can't always fear the incomplete;
sometimes with yourself you need to fight.

Closures are a full-stop;
don't confuse them with a comma.
Save yourself from the heartache
and the repetitive trauma.

What Is Your Deepest Desire She Asked

He replied:

What is your deepest desire?
What is it that sets your soul on fire?

Do you believe that you are born
with a specific purpose?
Or that you have a given role to play in life's circus?

On the surface I'm sure you'll find a long bucket list.
But I urge you to dig deeper coz
I'm sure something in the core does exist.

You know the exercise,
Take a deep breath and close your eyes.

Ask yourself again the same significant question,
The smile on your face says it all,
you don't need to mention!

In ~~love~~ sync with poetry!

The Story Untold

She wrote:

I will never look back to that story you told,
but come, it is time to let the mystery unfold.

He replied:

You've turned your back on me off late
and it's not a very good sight.
All colors seem lost right now;
my life has become black and white.

I count my blessings even then
and I'm glad you are still around.
You could have disappeared completely,
never to be found.

And hence, just before you board that train
to a land far far away.
I stand right behind you with a mandolin
wishing you'd show a sign and stay.

Wishing it would turn out exactly
the way it was foretold.
And you'd finally turn around and smile as it's time
to let the mystery unfold.

The White Dream

<u>She wrote:</u>

She is a dream you have to work hard for,
She is a dream yet you see it so clear.
She is a dream you strongly hoped for,
She is a dream you will always hold dear!

She is a dream that you want in the future,
She is a dream that you are eager to chase.
She is a dream that to your wounds is suture,
She is a dream you would kiss in grace!

In ~~love~~ sync with poetry!

He replied:

Her straight shiny hair not a single curl,
a dream so pure like a flawless deep-sea pearl.

The day so clear and well illuminated,
Time constraint limiting conversations
both new and back-dated.

Thus! Patience, hard work and
a strong hope for the future,
were all tiny prayers of the bigger picture!

This dream stood right there in front of his eyes,
dressed in white, an angel in disguise!

This angel however, was locked in her own spell.
She feared to dream of a tomorrow,
her hands in the pockets of past were held.

The only dream he was eager to chase,
The only dream he wanted destiny to kiss with grace.

But before anything of that took place,
He just wanted the angel to raise her head
and exchange "the forever gaze"

The Phoenix

<u>She wrote:</u>

I feel like a bird and you can't clip my wings.
I have giant dreams that can't be tied up with strings!

I want to have everything; I want to be free!
So what if I make choices unlike any of thee!

In ~~love~~ sync with poetry!

He replied:

A phoenix you are and you always will be,
It's a matter of time and I know you will see.

Your giant dreams and your quest of freedom,
Are all waiting with your crown
and your throne in your new kingdom.

Free, however, you first have to set yourself.
And I'm saying this once again
with the risk of repeating myself.

The tomorrow of forever that you've long been seeking.
You have it in sight; it's there, its waiting!

But first you'll have to set fire to your tragic past,
And then rise from the ashes
so you can make what truly matters, last!

Some Words That Need To Be Spoken

She wrote:

I trusted you so much as we spoke about our lives.
Your passionate touch and the love that filled our eyes!

Yet! We did not do much talking;
we did not say we care.
That's the beauty of it all, when love just fills the air.

There is no need to say in words,
your hearts deepest desire.
The deeds just feel enough,
there's warmth around that fire!

You know it when you go – just totally out of your way!
That this is the one for whom –
you want to do it all every day!

In ~~love~~ sync with poetry!

He replied:

The need to say it in words sometimes
is better than unshared desires,
to keep the flame burning always,
a forever supply of oxygen it requires.

Hence words spoken from the heart are nothing
but basic commitment of time,
the first good morning and the last good night to the
person that always stays on your mind.

And of course, once your words start rhyming,
your eyes start talking and silence suddenly
starts saying it all.
But before you let the heartbeats takeover,
make sure you've spoken about the fall!

The Missing Ice-Cream

She wrote:

With a smile as bright as sunlight,
and eyes with the depth of sea.

You lay down with her in the moonlight,
and forever that moment can be!

He replied:

Her eyes deeper than the ocean,
her smile brighter than the sun.
Catching hold of her is almost impossible;
she's always on the run!

A little promise to keep however,
she travelled across the seas,
Camping by the lakeside,
in a blue tent under the tall trees.

A teetotaler by choice she was
yet she ordered an Irish coffee.
Keeping her rule book aside for a day,
she knew she just wanted to be!

Her endless stories went on for hours;
she wanted him on the same page.
Secretly gazing into his eyes often,
some answers she was trying to gauge.

The sun vanished into the sky early;
it was a beautiful full moon night.
The reflection of the burning flames in the pit,
made her angelic eyes sparkle bright.

And just as he started staring into her eyes
laying under the moonlight,
Distracted once again, she sprang up in delight.

"It's time" she said,
"the perfect time to have the ice-cream"
The one thing he knew he'd forget,
which made him wake up from his dream.

The Warrior Disguised As A Princess

She wrote:

She is a warrior disguised as a princess.
She is all sane yet portrayed as a mess!

She is a killer disguised as a lover.
She is a woman you can never assess.

In ~~love~~ sync with poetry!

He replied:

Her disguises are plenty, yet! She is pure basic.
Too cautious when she approaches new territory,
to swim away she is very quick.

There's a reason why art and antique
is generally considered priceless,
Coz to the right person that desires them,
he'd never really want to assess.

The red carpet has been laid down for long;
the search is on for that perfect song.

When she could shed her every disguise,
And strike a pose with those sparkling eyes!

The only princess to rule all warriors,
walking proudly in a dress,
wearing her favorite sneakers.

The Mythical Goal

<u>She wrote:</u>

Run towards your GOAL,
drive with all your PASSION!
Love with your heart and SOUL,
dress and style with FASHION.

Walk like you are the BEST,
always keep that SMILE.
Even if you are placed among the REST,
Find a way to sprint that MILE!

In ~~love~~ sync with poetry!

He replied:

I've been walking tirelessly for months,
but haven't even covered a MILE,
I'd take this journey every single day though,
just to be able to see that SMILE.

Longer the road, clearer will the persistence be seen,
that is different from the REST.
It is surely worth the patience,
after-all it's for nothing but the BEST.

Being old school, acting like a fool
could seem to be out of FASHION.
But a pure reflex of the heart it is truly,
a path set by PASSION.

And hence, I continue walking every day
with my heart and SOUL,
Hoping that my prayers are answered one day,
when I'll walk down with my GOAL.

The Permanent Ink

<u>*She wrote:*</u>

He smiled, he hugged, he showed he cared.
But this sort of a relationship with
every person he shared.

I knew I got it wrong again, and it was just another day.
So I erased all of it in my head again,
I smiled, then looked away.

In ~~love~~ sync with poetry!

He replied:

He smiled, he hugged, he showed he cared.
And this sort of a relationship with quite a lot he shared.

Yet! Not a word from his treasures
of shushes he uttered or dared.
Often everything transparently in the open he bared.

Most days he kept praying whilst living the signs,
kept writing about his thoughts,
encrypting reality between the lines.

These lines were the ones to sense his heartbeat.
Not once but enough to let the story complete.

And yet his lines were erased and washed away,
His ink was permanent and he was here to stay.

The shadows of his lines stayed there forever,
Nothing felt the same or even close whatsoever.

The Carousel Called Life

<u>She wrote:</u>

Why do play in my head,
why do you run in my mind.

Why can't you love me with passion,
and let me experience human kind?

In ~~love~~ sync with poetry!

He replied:

Why do you play in my head,
why do you run in my mind?
I wish I could go back in time,
and relive our moments together in rewind.

In the amusement park of life,
we've literally shared every ride
We've lived the ups and downs together;
we've always been on each other's side.

It was until with the carousel that you wanted to explore,
letting you go was tough, I had never done that before.

But just as the ride started, I could finally see,
the farther you moved away
your eyes kept searching for me.

And after a few circles you finally did come around.
You have to lose yourself temporarily sometimes,
so that the forever can be found.

Why do you play in my head,
why do you run in my mind?
Keep enjoying the journey you are on,
you never know what you may find.

The Other Person

She wrote:

There is another person in my head,
and she answers to my name!

Sometimes she makes me doubt myself, also!
She messes with my brain.

He replied:

The other person in your head,
 the one that answers to your name.
The one that makes you doubt yourself,
doesn't let you feel the same.

This other person in your head that sits on the other side,
What if this person is actually trying to be your guide?

What if you opened up to the other person
and asked her what she really wants?
What if? The other person knows you better than you
think? And your most hidden desires she grants?

In ~~love~~ sync with poetry!

The Lemon Tree

She wrote:

I am eve and I am standing near a lemon tree.
Because I am not interested in apples anymore.

He replied:

They called me a misfit always,
a fruit yet tagged undesired and sour.
I kept my cool during most days,
doubt still managed to creep in every hour.

Why aren't you red like the other apples?
Mere words but to my soul they felt like shackles.

Fruit salads, fruit baskets, fruit custards
I was never a part of.
My tribe still believed in me,
even though I felt like a write off.

My creator, my mentor always
asked me to be and believe.
"You might not be the Adam of apples" my mum
had said, "but one day you will find your Eve"

A Heart Painted Blue

She wrote:

I stand like fire that can burn your soul,
my blood is fuel and heart is coal.

Amidst the darkness, the spark you ignite,
Has caused my life to stay forever bright.

I'm forbidden now to the human race,
there is an empty corner, with a lot of space.

Come fill my heart and paint it red,
Let's make this universe our love filled bed.

He replied:

Why would you say something and then look away?
Why do you keep disappearing but still want me to stay?

You claim to be forbidden to the human race,
whilst, to your destiny you secretly
keep praying to embrace.

You seem to have a thousand locks around your heart,
I promise to have a key for each one of them,
if you'd only let me start.

And once I'm let in, I can paint it for you.
Red it already is, I'd like to paint it blue.

The Rolling Dice

She wrote:

To engage with me, our eyes must talk!
Unending conversations and an endless walk!

When you think of me, if it brings a smile,
let's meet again, it's been a while.

I want to know if you feel insane.
And if you do, let's play this game.

Once the game is on, let's roll the dice,
let's mix it up – some sweet, some spice!

He replied:

Our words met first, my eyes were eager to talk.
Unending conversation lasted for a while
and a promise was made to take a beach walk.

My thoughts have been conquered;
it's surely been a while.
I now realize why I've had this forever smile.

I want to know too if insane is just enough.
Coz without knowing it, now my future looks tough.

I wish I could play it like any other game,
I've been stuck however, on that "very common name".

The crystals have foretold
about your destiny in disguise,
Do you still want them hidden
and rather trust the rolling dice?

The Phoenix – Redefined

She wrote:

You followed the trails of her dark mind;
she tried so hard to leave the mystery behind.

There was pain within that you failed to see,
she was tangled inside and wanted to be free.

She carried with her, the hurt and the pain.
When you let her go, it drove her insane.

The feeling so strong of what could have been,
a magical story that just went unseen.

It's a different kind of high – "The incomplete"
The reunion at another time that makes your heart beat!

In ~~love~~ sync with poetry!

He replied:

The love complete often dreads to thrive,
It is the incomplete that forever stays alive.

Crossroads move forward,
wider ways they often become,
the unfolding ways of destiny stays known to us seldom.

Let go, move on, set it free, I know says everybody.
The hurt, the pain however, can't be healed by nobody.

From your own ashes, Phoenix you gotta rise!
Give that hunch a chance; it could be a pleasant surprise.

If our rhymes have felt connected a lot many times,
I guess there's magic already,
I can almost hear the chimes!

Two Frozen Hearts

She wrote:

A poem that was never written,
a story that was never told.
I wonder what then got me smitten,
with love that felt passionate and bold.

Was it all those sweet talks, was it all those drives?
Was it all the story telling, or just your sympathy cries.

And now that you have chosen
to go back to what you were,
you left me out there frozen;
only wishing that you were here.

He replied:

The frozen wishes to talk to the frozen,
A lot of shattered out there are waiting to be chosen.

Chosen to be heard, healed and loved again!
Chosen to be able to live again.

Sure, your past was as beautiful as it could be,
it even might haunt you a certain night,
something from which you'd wish to be free.

Time heals all they say and I can see that now,
Destiny continues to surprise us often and how!

Don't stop, don't wait; take that leap of fate or faith!

Whatever you do don't lose that smile,
haven't seen something so pure, it's been a while!

Undefeated this spirit of yours I salute once again.
Forget the dark clouds, step out, open your arms –
Go! Dance in the rain!

The World's Smallest Lighthouse

Like a lighthouse she stood tall and strong,
always guiding others in the right direction,
protecting them from what was wrong.

Selfless, invested, to help others she always found time.
In the little that was left,
she'd tell stories wrapped in a rhyme.

Like a beacon her bright eyes
were visible from far miles,
many drifted towards her, attracted with just her smiles.

In ~~love~~ sync with poetry!

Everyone defined her existence
to merely be the guiding light,
Busy with touristy duties in the day,
saving lives by the night.

A wandering nomad who had lost
everything he once had in a storm,
Ran aground on the same island clueless
that his life was about to reform.

Whilst everyone applauded for what
the lighthouse had achieved,
the nomad noticed something that wasn't ever perceived.

Are you lost? He asked her. Your guiding light
always seems to be searching for something.
I know you've helped everyone around, yet in your eyes
I've looked, what are you truly seeking?

As soon as those magical words he uttered.
The princess was set free, an ancient curse shattered.

"You'd be locked until you find someone who'd
want you to find yourself first" was the spell.
A destiny written in the stars,
a fairytale for others to tell.

Kevin R Gandhi

Never Say Goodbye

Now that you've turned your back to me,
even with eyes in the clouds, I cannot see.

I cannot see on this step,
if you're waiting or walking away.
May be the ocean understands
how deeply I want you to stay.

Many stories of hope, destiny and love I have written.
The waves of time might erase them from the sand,
soon they'll be forgotten.

And hence today, I'd like to etch something on the sky.
Who else can best teach us
that there's never a Goodbye?

The sun you bid adieu to tonight!
Will be back again tomorrow shining bright!

In ~~love~~ sync with poetry!

The Forbidden Fruit

She wrote:

I'm the story of the forbidden fruit,
of depth and meaning and a bitter truth.

I just need one reason to run that mile;
I just need one moment to make me smile.

Love hurts me now, but can I do it again?
I hate the storm, but I also want the rain.

I'm giving up on poetry; I'm giving up on rhyme.
Come fix this up when you have the time.

He replied:

Prayers speak louder than words,
so I think on this one I'll choose to remain mute.
Yet, somehow, I then heard the singing birds,
hinting that my calling's been the forbidden fruit.

The depth and meaning of life,
we all seek out to understand.
Not realizing that it's limited, running out of our hands
we hold tight, like a pile of fine sand.

Leave the reasons alone for the brain to wonder on,
Trust your heart, travel a thousand miles
if you have to, go wander on.

Nestled far away on the other side
of the world it could be,
That moment, the reason for your
forever smile you could see.

Love hurts a lot, from my own wounds I can tell.
But somehow heals better every time
with its magic spell.

And as you grow older, a bit wiser you begin to get.
And that's when you realize
how often you tend to forget.

That pure love doesn't confine,
it in fact sets you free,
It is the expectations that hurt
and don't let you be.

In ~~love~~ sync with poetry!

The Heart And The Mind Still Don't Sync

She wrote:

I can't think, and I can't write,
my heart and mind don't sync, they just fight.

The choice I made, the path I chose,
is my vision still blurry?
On each step its thorns and foes.

Why don't you write, a little story again for me,
a new story of hope, with better destiny.

He replied:

I could write you a fresh long story,
For an Nth number of time.
I could spend sleepless hours again
and even get it to rhyme.

Yet! An answer to your question
I'm not sure if I can help you find.
Its rhetoric nature indeed I can point
out if you'd let me rewind.

So you say your heart and mind don't sync
and they just seem to fight?

And then you feel reading a story with hope
or about destiny will set it right?

Hope and destiny both will
never make sense to the mind,
the heart won't rest until what it wants,
it finally is able to find.

So more than hope and destiny
I feel the story now needs clarity,
the timeline has been rewritten on a fresh page,
and the situation is overflowing with gravity!

A good thing about choices is that
they can be made every single day
and if a path you've taken makes you feel lost -
wander again, You might just find your forever way!

And whilst the unexpected wind might
seem to blemish the flawless style,
I see those eyes still locked with the lens
and the perfection in that smile.

The determination in those eyes is
the "hope" you want to see,
and that smile on the face is your faith on destiny.

And thus, the story that you seek
 is within for you to find.
Listen to your heart always
and simply let the mind follow behind.

In love sync with poetry!

Just Like That

She wrote:

And just like that, it was over.

He replied:

And just like that, it was over.
It passed pretty fast, but felt a little slower.

I kept waiting on the other side of the river,
whilst he built the bridge persistently and crossed over!

Over the deep waters of doubt,
Over the constant pressure to back out.

Over the yesterday's and over the pain.
Over the logic that questioned the again.

And just like that, it was over.
That never ending wait for my forever!

The Dream Car

She wrote:

I'm in love with you, why don't you
tell me who you are?
I'm in love with you; you make me feel like a star!

I'm in love with you,
because we've rhymed and come this far.
You're in love with me?
Okay then, it's time to buy me a car!

He replied:

The car I am considering is a convertible and it's blue,
It's beautiful indeed, yet! Nothing compared to you.

It's got a starlight panoramic roof too,
But who's gonna need that, sitting right next to you.

I've planned a long road trip,
mostly taking the scenic route by the sea.
We can sing a few songs or
you could just rhyme alone with me.

I'll also pack an elaborate picnic coz I know
you'd be hungry on the way.
We can pop up the roof, gaze at the view,
be it the middle of the night or day.

I've chosen the best spot on a high cliff
to watch the sun setting in the ocean,
Probably click a few memories with you adoring the
orange sun, the cool breeze and
that content smile all in slow motion.

All set! I'm here to pick you up and just
as I reach out to grab your side of the door,
Wow! What a dream I tell myself, with a million dollar
smile still lying injured on the floor!

The Beast with a Human Heart

She wrote:

Why do you play with my head,
why do you run in my mind?
Why can't you love me with passion?
And let me experience human kind.

Human kind isn't easy, they play hard to get.
They don't value what they have,
and when they lose it, they regret.

He replied:

Body of a beast, soul of the human kind.
Cursed by circumstances, He often searched
for himself, yet couldn't find!

Cast away in a dark cave of agony,
a long pursued dream had kept him alive.
He also once wanted just love with passion,
somewhere! He still wanted it to thrive.

His humane was snatched away,
yet! He felt something after a long long time.
He wasn't playing hard to get at all;
all those rhymes were surely his dose of enzyme!

Naked a beast would still be a beast,
he wanted the beauty to see his human side,
Hence, he had faith that at the right time
their destinies will coincide!

The Complicated Clues

She wrote:

Now that I am here, where do I start?
With the Trapp Family Singers – or Mozart?

I looked around. Thought I recognized a Youtuber.
But not you. So I waited, like Liesl for her Rolfe Gruber.

I then went down to the Makarsteg Bridge.
A pretty picture, for a magnet on your fridge.

Did I leave you my heart in a lock?
You'll have to look very carefully to see.

If you find it, it will be a shock,
But a good one I'll give you the key.

So come find me, But only if you really fell.
Where? The place is heaven but sounds like "hell".

In ~~love~~ sync with poetry!

He replied:

I digitally roamed around the streets of Salzburg.
Your clues for some reason
are just the tip of the iceberg.

I did lend an ear to the creations of
both the trap family and Mozart,
Yet! It's tough to say what exactly
goes around in a poet's heart.

Leisl loved right but I find Rolfe to be worldly wrong.
I highly doubt his genuineness
and even the sweet 16 song!

Enjoying the subtle evening breeze,
I walked right up to the Makartsteg Bridge.

Locks of today have multiple keys,
the modern urge for practicality; I see it as a disease.

I'd rather walk north for another 7 minutes
to reach the place I think I will find.
The picturesque palace that will place
eternal time on rewind.

Altenau castle! It originally was supposed to be called.
Where true love blossomed, against all evils, it sprawled.

This hunt, the treasure, the history,
I ain't sure yet of what I seek.
I've travelled all the way around,
to find out more, to understand, to speak!

Every City Has Its Own Love Story

She wrote:

Every city has its love story,
like its own food and fashion.
Even in the stoniest heart,
there rages cold and hot passion.

The singer Constance Weber and
Wolfgang Amadeus Mozart.
Archbishop Wolf Dietrich and the beautiful Salome Alt.

As an expression of love, there are few that are finer
Than Constance's solo soprano
for Mozart's great mass in C minor.

Salome was the love of the Archbishop Dietrich's life
He built Mirabell palace for her,
but she could never be his wife.

But it seems that my own great story
hasn't yet been written.
You know that old saying: twice shy when once bitten!

Because I experienced a gush of love,
but it never ever stayed.
My fate deceived me, and I always felt betrayed.

So I am alone but secure, in my isolated lair.
But they say there's always hope,
and may be a little prayer.

In ~~love~~ sync with poetry!

He replied:

Every city has its own love story,
like its own food and fashion.
Only a few names remain in glory, Even though every
soul that lived, loved at least once with passion.

We all tend to build a Mirabell
in our hearts for our Salome.
A handful few are lucky with a forever,
Rest! With or without somebody are still left alone.

Luckiest are the ones who in-spite of losing it all,
Choose to rise again and forget their past fall.

Your final great story has surely been written,
once time has healed all, you'll surely be smitten!

Yet! Away from that bridge, you will have to be.
Where love was kept locked up without its sanctity!

And once you walk away, not very far you shall see,
a clear flowing river, as free as it could be!

It is here where you'll begin, to love without fear.
As rare as it is, to find an earring on that ear!

The Princess without Her Crown

She wrote:

Often we misunderstand her, often we choose to judge.
When she knows she is real,
she will never choose to budge.

She has had the worst of events;
she has had the best of times.
She loves to tell her stories;
she loves to call them Rhyme's.

In ~~love~~ sync with poetry!

He replied:

Cast under the shadow of her tragic past.
Tied to the strings of attachment that wouldn't last.

Yet! Hopeful with her head high
she would still daydream,
only if she listened more often to the voice on her team.

Draped in black from head to toe,
For the sake of her forever,
she turned every friend into Foe!

Yes! She was often misunderstood,
often chosen to be judged.
With a heavy heart she carried,
she could hardly walk, she often trudged!

Her rhymes that kindled a heartbeat somewhere,
were suddenly a thing of the past,
her stories vanished, not to be found anywhere!

Out there in the scorching heat of ambiguity,
He waited on the roads for days, it was such a pity!

Yet! Holding the ladder of life,
strongly he chose to wait.
A strong foundation he knew was needed,
everything else he could leave to fate.

He kept singing the songs of a better tomorrow
each day multiple times.

Kept revisiting her stories,
words from her own fairytale rhymes.

Stranded on the top of that ladder he knew she felt,
Too numb to climb any further, too sceptic
to come down, yet alone with it she dealt.

Any haste on his part to bring her down,
He knew he'd than have the princess without her crown.

Hence, patiently he chose for her
to know when it felt right.
Coz once she knows it's real,
she'll jump for it with all her might.

And down below he knew,
he was always ready to make the catch,
at a place she never approved to be,
destiny still gave her an exceptional match!

In ~~love~~ sync with poetry!

Look Into My Eyes

She asked:

What do you see when you look into my eyes?

He replied:

When I look into your eyes, there's an ocean I can see!
I can somehow read the sorrows,
live every known memory!

When I look into your eyes, there's an ocean I can see!
Staring at a stream of stories, a flowing reflection of me.

I think we've met before,
watched the sunset along the seashore.

It's like an everlasting Déjà vu,
as if I've always known you!

When I look into your eyes, there's an ocean I can see!
I forget to blink my eyes, never imagined,
this silly I could be!

There is something I see beyond,
a connection deeper than the sea.
Liked the waves, I keep smiling.
Amazed at this mystery.

Nothing else seems to distract me now,
from my pain you've set me free!
I've always believed in fairytales, in the power
of the universe and as much in Destiny!

When I look into your eyes, there's an ocean I can see.
Like a dream on a starry night,
only waiting for you to look at me!

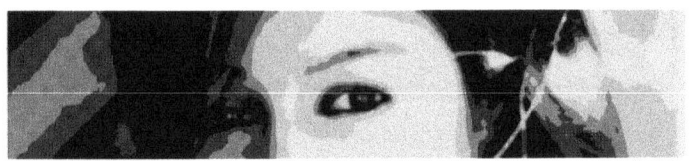

In ~~love~~ sync with poetry!

The Swansong

~~~~~~~~~~

She wrote:

This is not a swansong,
but I'm hoping someday there will be!
A swansong so romantic,
writing in poetry back to me!

He replied:

Ever wondered why upon checking into a hotel room
a couple of swan shaped towels you see?
Easily done it's also coz they mate for life and
with each other forever they will be.

"Forever" a word that both over and ever it contains.
And principally, to live through both, "the over"
and "the misfit ever" it pains.

And yet! We choose to wait all our lives
for that swansong.
Coz we all inherently want to be at a place
where we truly belong.

And if there's anything in poetry that
I as the swan upon retiring could sing to you,
I'd stare into your eyes, with your smile be mesmerized
and just ask you to be true.

True to yourself, to your dreams and your worth.
As there's nothing above being romantic to yourself,
in heaven or on this earth.

In ~~love~~ sync with poetry!

Alice In Wonderland

She wrote:

Red hat, blue skies, water but no sand.
What would you say to this Alice in wonderland?

He replied:

Red hat, blue skies, water! But no sand.
Easily an addiction, very tough to comprehend.

Alice! She loved her dreams where she could just be,
She loved wandering too and
specifically her favorite ginger tea!

A golden heart, nerves of steel
and eyes deeper than the sea.
To watch her lost in her own world and happy,
a dreamland of its own it would be.

To meet her in person an opportunity, if I ever had,
I'd tell her, "We're all mad here, I'm mad, you're mad"

In ~~love~~ sync with poetry!

A Story To Remember

She wrote:

The day you give me a story I would never forget.
I will give you my company with zero regret.

He replied:

This is a story about a charming mermaid princess.
She lived life on her terms and about
the world's opinion, she cared less.

Swimming back to her oyster palace on a random day,
she noticed something dropped from the sky above
and it came drifting her way.

It was a bright red leaf which looked very unique,
Mysteries like these to solve,
she would always impulsively seek.

The next few days she swam to the corners of the sea,
In search of similar red leaves or
from wherever it could be.

She felt a deep connection with the bright red leaf;
it somehow resonated with her core basic belief.

The next day she woke up,
she noticed something magical.
The leaf she had preserved had a story glowing on it
and with her dreams it was identical.

The story on the leaf continues to be a mystery till date;
however, it was good enough for the princess to move
to the magical land without any further wait.

In ~~love~~ sync with poetry!

A Vow Not Taken
and
A Wow Mistaken

This smile! So rare, is back and I don't know how?
I can't seem to break away from your gaze,
and I'm playing with my hair now?

How is it that I can't deny the signs that I see?
Why am I so caught up in what was and what will be?

You secretly managed to crawl into my dreams;
you bribed me to smile talking about
coffees and ice creams.

You strive a lot to be a part of my busy days,
with feathers, pebbles and leaves
you've always found your ways.

My heartbeats seem to respond to your rhymes,
I smile every time I hear the melodic chimes.

This smile! So rare is back and I don't know how?
I am still smiling as I type this;
"You managed to do it again! Wow!"

Kevin R Gandhi

In ~~love~~ sync with poetry!

Part II

Kevin R Gandhi

Hey There Sunshine: 26ᵗʰ July 2020

Hey there! Sunshine!
Thank God! I waited in line.

Behind the clouds of doubt you stayed for long,
Yet, I just knew that you'd come along!

Glad! I believed in the powers of the universe,
mysteriously, my words turned into verse,

The tent, the coffee maker and the telescope,
we'll all be waiting by this lake,
our hearts filled with hope.

In ~~love~~ sync with poetry!

I've been walking alone on this journey for miles,
on the way encountering a few glances and wide smiles.

Yet! I am unable to stay at any one place;
I've been seeking you without your trace.

I've packed my bag with patience and persistence,
set out to discover you and your existence.

And even though I am clueless about this road
and to where it would lead,
something within wants me to try with all my heart,
Tells me, I am destined to succeed!

And hence, Sunshine! I shall continue to walk,
hoping I make it, beyond the 12' o clock!

Kevin R Gandhi

The Miracle Unicorn

You're neither a goat nor a horse she was told,
Deemed a misfit, they banished her to suffer in the cold.

No one saw her pure healing qualities,
or that she could turn anything she wished into gold.
Not until her magical horn remained visible,
Or miraculous stories about her started to unfold.

And whilst you may feel an urge
for her to get back at them,
she was merely busy building her own kingdom
of dreams, commanding the helm!

Now, famously known as the miracle unicorn,
what was mocked earlier; became the unique symbol
of her magic, her single horn!

Yet! Away from everything she now wanted to be,
Numb with pain within, she wanted to break free.

She dreamt of a paradise often
which was far across the seas,
where rainbows laid like flowers on the ground,
and the stars danced around them like bees.

Where the sun followed the road shinning
through the trees.
And waterfalls retraced into winds,
turning mist into magical breeze.

A leap of faith she knew she had to take,
A few changes within she knew she had to make.

After all that she felt, she just had to try,
the wings she never knew she had,
Would then make her fly!

She was the magic all along,
just needed "somebody" to show it to her,
that somebody that would love her forever, not!
Anybody in a shining armor!

And so we conclude that the fairytale
is always in your hands,
not in magic, or casts or spells or carved stone bands!

The Mermaid - Defined: 22nd August 2020

She swims around with her big dreamy eyes;
her habit of day dreaming may take you by surprise!

Very intuitive, she can beat the world's best spies,
there's always more to her, than what meets the eyes!

And don't be fooled by the look of her size,
She's Din Lino in Nemo's disguise.

She would swim against strong currents
to help a loved one out;
ironically, it's her own little troubles
that she can never figure out.

Going with the flow comes naturally to her,
but she's got a stubborn angle too,
that no soul can conquer.

Very unique and a rare sight to find,
The beautiful mermaid living amongst us humankind!

In ~~love~~ sync with poetry!

The Mighty Waterfall

You keep flowing endlessly, it's tough to keep a track,
I'm still going to walk alongside,
till you find your way back.

On these trails we've shared stories for hours,
And yet! Time still feels to fall short.
There's so much to catch up on,
and a lot that we have to sort.

The sound of your flow is like music to my ears,
without it even a few minutes somehow
feel like lifeless long years!

I can't stop at this shallow stream,
I want to know about every nightmare, every dream.

I know where I've reached hasn't
even been accessible to all,
I somehow feel we're connected deeper,
And hence, I've set out to seek you,
Even if I have to get behind the mighty waterfall!

In ~~love~~ sync with poetry!

The Child in Her:

This child in her she'd like to keep,
a lioness siting in the hide of a sheep.

This child in her that believes in fairy tales,
Shares interesting stories with in-depth details.

This child in her that makes a peculiar face,
On finding food she doesn't like,
after she's done saying grace.

This child in her that has innocence alive, in her
entrancing eyes and ravishing smile.
The child that loves sleeping for hour's together
coz honestly, it's been a while.

"Grow up!" "Act your age!" We're all advised,
whilst this little child in us is victimized.
Our dreams are turned into meaningless life goals,
and the believing spirit within is sanitized.

Don't be afraid to let the child out and let it play.
After all! We're all just temporary here;
we're all just dolls made of clay!

Our First Coffee Meet: 21ˢᵗ Nov

Our first coffee meet, we sat at different tables.
Ordered different drinks with our individual labels.

A little mix-up of the orders, Got us to meet.
I still ain't sure about sharing this story,
Or about keeping it discreet.

Who would've thought our paths
would cross again a few times,
and eventually our stories would be shared
with your pictures and my rhymes!

In ~~love~~ sync with poetry!

The Little Blue Fish

"I am going back" she told him ,
It's about time I stop chasing the "silly" dream.

In a moment her whole life
like a story flashed in his mind,
Helpless he felt as answers to her questions;
he wasn't able to help her find.

They'd met not very recently on the
crossroads of their journey.
Scars they both had, their independent
pasts had been thorny.

A part of each other's destiny, He just knew they were.
Signs so often otherwise wouldn't always appear.

Friends forever they'd been it always felt,
some moments he knew, he'd never be able to forget.

And then suddenly a lot like strangers he felt,
how could he not remember
that they'd actually never "met"?

"Why would you quit your pursuit halfway?"
He asked her. "Why would you return to the Dead Sea?"
Wouldn't you for life be restless?
To know what could your life really be?

"These questions are the exact reason!" she told him.
"I am just tired of everything you see?"
"Tired you aren't with the questions, little blue fish"
he told her. Tired you are from being
who you wouldn't want to be!

And don't take a word from this
wandering stranger you don't know,
But you'd listen to your own heartbeats although?

For years you've neglected the heart
and worked like a machine.
I know that pain, like you exactly know what I mean.
And not just me but every soul
with whom for a lifetime you have been.

Has only just asked you to dare
this one last time to dream.
After all! them, me and you, we're all on the same team.

Yes! You loved the person so dearly in the past.
In spite of how you were made to feel like an outcast.

Yes! I know this person still and
will always mean a lot to you,
But dear to avoid the pain
you can't "try to love" a statue.

Contd..........

In ~~love~~ sync with poetry!

The statue sure is an idol of what
everyone else couldn't be.
But the missing that never was,
how do you plan to find so suddenly?

Anyway! You've always found a way and you
will this time too, in YOU I trust.
When you can't figure out what you clearly want.
What you don't! You need to strike off, you must!

You're a fish after all you might
not be able to think straight.
Go for it, be lost for one last time, take a full circle
again, for you once more I shall patiently wait!

The Mermaid and
The Lost Sailor

This story about a mermaid and the lost sailor
seems long forgotten like an unfinished movie
with an exceptional trailer.

The sailor was led to the mermaid
under unusual circumstances,
and it was very rare for the mermaid to have
taken such exceptional chances.

"You're a wanderer. How can I trust
that you'll ever settle down?"
Besides! We come from different worlds she added.
"I'm ashore only for two days until
I find my magical crown"

They spoke different languages
yet understood the same melody,
to their strong belief in destiny this was indeed a parody.

"You seem familiar" he told her.
"If not home yet, I surely feel very near."

"Let's just get to know each other a bit better,
you're free to return to your world, and if you'd
still want to know more, write me a letter"

They lost track of time and
told each other a lot about their lives,

In ~~love~~ sync with poetry!

He almost got her to wish Good mornings every day
and she taught him to wink with both eyes.

Days passed by, they managed to keep in touch
with different means.
He felt she was drifting away trying
to balance multiple reigns.

The more patient he got,
the less time they managed to get,
He still kept writing to her; reminding in different ways
of why there had to be a reason that they'd met!

A few weeks of waiting she sent him
a message from down below,
I need to do some searching alone and this time
I won't even come up to say "hello"!

With a smile on his face he dived deep
to see her one last time,
holding his breath till eternity to see if in her world,
he could still feel the rhyme.

Once you've found yourself come see me by the shore.
Wear these magical stones around your hand and you
won't have to swim in the unknown anymore.

A few days later at sunset her flukes vanished
as she stood on her feet,
with the magical stones around her wrist hoping
this time with the sailor "forever" she will meet!

Wishes And Dreams

If you had to pick between your wishes
and your dreams" she asked him,
"Which one would you choose?"
That question sure did get him wondering.
An answer he knew, he couldn't refuse.

Thinking deeper he asked himself, "Does a dream
eventually turn into a wish?" "Or do you start
dreaming about your wishes eventually?"
A paradox that he just couldn't resolve fully.

Thinking about her then,
he did manage to get some clarity.
Answering her question with a smile he said,
"You are both for me you see,
and even if only one I then have to choose,
WE will one day be a reality!"

In ~~love~~ sync with poetry!

Different Worlds:

They belonged to different worlds,
yet! Shared the same dream.
A lake, a tent and a picnic with coffee,
wine and sugar free ice cream.

A promise often he made to her,
to protect her dreams both seen and unseen.
She wanted to trust his promises often,
but for a long time hidden in a shell she had been.

Queen of the ocean she was, she ruled the
blue waters and everything it did encompass.
And yet, often times than ever she drooled on thoughts
that challenged her assumed purpose.

Explorer of the skies he was, Raw, unashamed and free.
Yet! Worthy of her list of a hundred things
he told her he could be.

"One day!" he told her, "I shall see you where
the ocean and the sky meet"
Until then, with open eyes too,
this dream I'll keep playing on repeat.

Kevin R Gandhi

Stories on the Rocks

In ~~love~~ sync with poetry!

"I don't get you!" she once said to him acting surprised.
"How can you be so patient and persistent?"
"That's the only way I know" he said,
looking into her curious eyes.

"The universe grants you what's truly yours
when you're consistent, you see!" These stories
on the rocks weren't carved in a day.
We marvel at these sights centuries later,
after nature found its destined way!

"I keep flowing endlessly like that waterfall" she said,
"I have no time, I cannot stay!"
"I'll be that colorful rainbow around you" he said,
staring into those innocent eyes.
"But I will forever find a way!"

I Shall Send You A Sign

"How are you so imaginative?"
she asked him, making time to keep
their endangered conversation alive.
"Aren't we the same in that case?"
He murmured. Reminding her how she
could weave stories when she was only five.

"You're already everything you wanted to be"
he continued. "You see! It's just that
you don't get enough time"
"Play often, catch up on those hours of missing sleep"
he added, May be take a break to rhyme.

In ~~love~~ sync with poetry!

"I'm like the waves of the ocean" she explained.
"I can't take a break, I have to keep it going"
"You're right! You'll always be."
He acknowledged. "How about reinventing your pace and consider well! Slowing?"

"Life is also about balance" he highlighted.
"The waves at some point Might be taken for granted"

"I want it all on some days" she exclaimed.
"I wish a miracle I could find"
"It's already within you" he told her.
"And to finally begin,
I SHALL SEND YOU A SIGN!"

A Sunflower without its Sunshine

"You hardly know her, she's technically still a stranger"
someone told him trying to prepare
him about the potential danger.

"This is how the heart beats"
he said smiling. "It doesn't consider the
what, when, who and how. It just beats."

"What do you mean?" The person asked
again with a confused look.
"You see! Matters of the heart can't follow
steps mapped by the brain on a book"

"Do you see those sunflowers?" he asked,
wanting to explain what he meant in detail.
"Without their 'sunshine' they won't feel the same
anymore, they'll turn extremely pale"

"And just like that! The Sun will rise
and set on its own time.
Yet for the sunflower, rising without its sunshine
will feel like a crime"

In ~~love~~ sync with poetry!

Set Me Free

"I am addicted to your smile and your voice,
I wish we could talk everyday"
he told her after their brief conversation on the phone.
"I don't usually catch up with people" she replied,
being cutely honest. "I think I best work alone"

"Besides! I've survived a major lockdown already"
She added. "Not sure to feel locked
up again if I'm ready"

"From the ashes, I've revived and through
it all alone I've survived. "I am unsure
about walking down the flames again;
I'd rather enjoy it alone flying in the rain"

"You see!" he interrupted. "For centuries now love
has been portrayed with a lock and key,
when in reality it is true love that indeed sets you free."

"And in no way I ever want your flight to be affected.
I just want you to see the sky you deserve and that smile
I want protected"

"I also know that flying together is a distant dream
and that your heart is like a non-melting ice cream."

"Yet! I believe even with these stitched wings that I can
fly, and that together one day, we will share our blue
sky"

Kevin R Gandhi

When It Rained From the Ground

"On a scale of 1-10, how much do you think you like me?" he asked her, keeping his fingers crossed.
Hoping that this doesn't end up like the
many questions she's previously tossed.

"I don't! You're at -3" she replied on a text,
probably with a 'Duchenne smile' on her face.
Impairing his attempts to step up their rare
conversations and pick up some pace.

"Imagine this..." he tried continuing
the broken conversation.
"I don't believe in the hypotheticals" she said
interrupting again, changing the situation.

He just knew that she was hiding something in her heart.
He'd been feeling it all along, right from the very start.

"I can see that smile you know" he then replied.
Telling her somehow, he knew and that
the obvious was implied.

"How can you be so sure?" she asked him.
"Did you see any other signs?"
Knowing that he's made references about them,
many a times.

In ~~love~~ sync with poetry!

"What if I show you one right away?"
he asked her, almost sensing her smiling again.
"What?" She replied with a devil smiley
"On a hot sunny day are you gonna make it rain?"

"I'd rather show you" he replied
and then initiated a video call.
That was the only way he could see that smile after all.

He was sitting on a wooden bench facing the sea.
Clear skies, blue waters,
the day as beautiful as it could be.

"What now?" She teased him again.
"Not a single cloud in the sky!" she exclaimed.

And just as she said that, a sudden gust of water burst
out of the deck where he was at!
"That's a sign. Isn't it?" He asked.
"No smarty! Timing it just is"
she said and cleverly passed.

"Gotta go! Sorry, I'm late for my call!" she said
smirking and she hung up without saying goodbye.
With his head down in vain, he started
walking away from the deck with a long sigh.

Just then, he saw something, his eyes sparkled,
heartbeats raced as his smile grew broader.
A little sign lying beside the fountain
read it was currently "Out of Order"

Legend Of The P'quals

"There is a situation going out here. Sorry! I've been
out of sight" She said, apologizing about things
that were out of her control.
"Don't worry about it. Please don't be sorry" he said.
"I get you! Not just in pieces but as a whole!"

"And just like Kuekuatsu looks up in the sky and howls
her name every night" he continued.
"Until they wander the skies together,
I too shall be glued"

"How can you be so sure?" She asked him.
"Why would you walk alone this far for someone?"
Pointing towards the board with legend
of the P'quals on it he said,
"Not for someone no! But surely for THE ONE!"

"So you see" he continued. "You can't let your
mind run the matters of the heart"
"For 'the one' you could walk half way across
the earth and that'll still be the easy part!"

In ~~love~~ sync with poetry!

Learn the Flow

"I'm sure you don't want to make 26 attempts"
she said teasing him about his upcoming test.
"26? I've made a lot more than 260 by now"
he replied hoping his wit will leave her impressed.

"Timing again, smarty!" she said smiling timidly
wanting to avoid the later part of the conversation.
Patient he always was, persistent off lately
he'd become for a confrontation.

"Shush!" read her next text without an additional line.
A smiley along with it though
would have been an apt sign.

"Our boat is going around in circles"
he reminded her after a while.
"Circles? The boat? How?"
she asked teasing him again hiding her smile.

"Well! You see it's just one paddle
that is consistently moving ahead.
The other one is either going backwards or to move
together it seems scared" he said.
"And then it wouldn't matter how far
this paddle would want them to go.
They'll just keep going around in circles
until together they learn to flow"

A Boat from My Sunset to Your Sunrise

I wish a boat I could hail and travel
from my sunset to your sunrise.
I wish a few rules I could break, land outside
your door and well! Scream "surprise!"

I wish I could expand our brief conversations into days,
and to shrink the years when you're busy into a few
seconds, I wish there were ways.

I wish super smart you'd stop acting for a while,
in the cameras we joke about, I wish
I actually could see you smile.

I wish with my never-ending jokes
I could make you laugh all the time
and for when you feel "fed up"; I could
maybe write you a cheerful rhyme.

In ~~love~~ sync with poetry!

I wish more time at hand we had,
to exchange our consistent dreams,
So more things I could finally add to the list with
the lakes, coffees and ice creams.

I could wish for this and I could wish for that.
And it might feel that I'm changing the fish's habitat.

And that's probably why a wish I first want you to make,
If that huge step of getting onboard
you finally want to take.

Matched By Destiny

"Are you counting the signs?" He asked
her keeping his fingers crossed again.
"Just another coincidence!" She said.
"You can't take credits for the rain"

"And what if for the rain someone's
prayed with all his heart?"
"Wished and hoped for it both,
with devotion right from the start?"

He asked and continued. "What if
it started raining out of the blue?"
"Some stories run parallel for a long time until
they suddenly become one; who knew?"

"Just like this bridge that surely wasn't built in a day!"
"The circle of life will ensure,
what is destined will find its way"

"Oh wait! That reminds me"
Interrupting she asked abruptly.
"Two circles, is that a Visa or MasterCard?"
"Fast! I am on the payment page, Answer me quickly!"

"MasterCard!" He said, smiling incessantly.
Feeling proud that they were indeed matched by destiny!

In ~~love~~ sync with poetry!

Wrecks Can Be Beautiful Too

Wrecks can be beautiful too!
An interesting story they often have to tell.
Living proofs they are of certain things
in life not going too well.

Yet! It's totally possible to paint your wreck,
Think out of the box and escape that bottleneck.

Have an entire forest to look like your backyard,
The rivers as your pools and the trees as your sun guard.

And as long as this quest is enough to make you happy.
Senseless to the world you can seem
or be tagged as the "unapologetic hippie"

Scars can be beautiful too;
you shouldn't feel a need to keep them concealed.
Just take good care of them,
make sure from within they are healed.

Sometimes the only way to find yourself;
is to first get completely lost.
And remember that, what is truly yours
will always remain, Always! At any cost!

In ~~love~~ sync with poetry!

The Genie He Found In the Sea

Genie: I can grant you to be something or someone else. What would you wish to be?
Him: Work!
Genie: Wait what? Work?
Him: Yes! I'd wish to be "this work"
that she spends all her time with.

I'd wish to be that first cup of Ginger tea she looks forward to hang out with.
I'd wish to be the furry friend that makes her mundane day lit.

I'd wish to be "the shower" she uses as an excuse to avoid few conversations.
I'd wish to be the document she reviews so meticulously with all the explanations.

I'd wish to be that specific desert, the only
thought of which is enough to bring a broad smile.
I'd wish to be that movie she's been wanting to watch,
but hasn't been able to for a while.

I'd wish to be that bowl of hot steamy noodles
she craves for, after midnight.
I'd wish to be the dream she's fond of seeing
with open eyes that keeps reality out of sight.

Genie: Woah! Woah! Woah! Just one!
Please pick just one.

Him: You know what?
I'd wish to be in the middle of that sea
and if it's truly meant to be, this time!
Let her come looking for me.

In ~~love~~ sync with poetry!

Shades of Blue

I keep wandering to discover these
different shades of blue,
the best ones I look forward to revisit with you!

Our connection has been very tidal for some time;
you're gone for days without a word or even a rhyme.

And a storm might seem to uproot me from the ground,
but along your banks my traces will eternally be found.

Only when the waves settle will
you be able to clearly see.
We're not strangers anymore,
slowly becoming one, you and me!

Don't Miss the Train

It's been a while since we crossed
paths at the train station.
It's been a while since we discovered that we're headed
to the same destination.

It's been a while that we've exchanged stories
and stargazed the whole night.
It's been a while since we caught up "out of the blue";
you've almost been out of sight.

In ~~love~~ sync with poetry!

My solo journey without your company
now seems quite boring.
Questions about "our story" from all directions
now seem to be soaring.

And I know taking a step doesn't
come to you quite naturally.
And tough it's gonna be for me too, to do it virtually.

It's been a while that my heartbeats
have agreed to every visible sign,
It's been a while that I've felt my destiny did intertwine.

Hence! To make sure that the story written
by the stars does not go in vain.
I'll have to come and get you,
stretch my hand once again;
just to make sure that you don't miss this train!

Just Coincidences or True Signs?

"I am tempted to be on the other side" he said.
"How long will I be the werewolf who
endlessly stares at the moon?"
"Don't cross that bridge yet!" she said.
"You know that I'm gonna be there very soon"

"This fierce river of time keeps flowing between us"
he opined.
"These signs that you keep shunning as coincidences,
in reality, are very tough to find"

"No! Don't haste it" she almost commanded.
"Why are you suddenly in such a rush?"
"Suddenly?" he asked surprisingly.
"I would still tell you but then you'll ask me to shushh!"

"Go ahead! Tell me" she said nudging him playfully.
"I appreciate honesty the most"
"Well!" he stated nervously.
"How else am I gonna take it to the next step,
sitting on another coast?"

"I can almost see you and hear
you just fine from here" she replied.
"Exactly! I wanted to change this
almost and the just fine" he sighed

"Yet! Once again. I'll patiently wait for
my moon and your sun to get aligned.
Hoping the forgotten inner voices in us, these
'coincidental' signs can help us find!"

Old V/S New

"I don't know this 'old you' that you
dearly keep talking about" she said.
"I've only gotten to know you better
in these recent years!"
A ruminating thought dived deep down his soul,
as soon as those words reached his ears.

His old battered soul that was healing
in hibernation, was it truly lost?
And if it indeed did evolve, He'd need to
figure that out at any cost.

He thought his boat was anchored
even though free it was to move in its own space.
He thought on a voyage he'd set out
and get rid of the futile rodent race.

He was unsure of how his explorations,
would taint his core conscience.
He just believed that with time he'd get there,
trusting his patience and persistence.

Buried in these thoughts,
he silently bid adieu to the setting sun.
Wondering how the man of last words was
suddenly left with none.

"Actions often speak louder than words"
he concluded. "I'll wait until this 'new me'
feels to seem a lot like the old"
"Honesty will always remain the best policy
and so does the purity of gold."

"Until then these conversations we will continue,
hoping my words can spread some charms.
And if a library full of words still feels incomplete,
you'll still find me waiting with open arms.

A Rhyme Incomplete

I know you're out there
your heartbeats I can hear.
We're thousands of miles apart,
yet! You've always felt near.

The faster I try to chase you,
farther you just drift away.
Free flowing like the waves you are, Yet! certain I am,
one day forever you'll choose to stay!

Distance! It is said is the essence of some stories,
until ready they are to transcend,
the clenching territories.

And whilst another evolving rhyme
with new words I can repeat,
This one with a question for you
I am leaving, hoping you'll find some time to make it complete.
What should we only talk about when we finally meet?

In ~~love~~ sync with poetry!

My Heart Beats In the Sea

"Stay away! For your own good".
He was told, "You're a wanderer and she's a mermaid"
It's doesn't matter how it all started
or how eternal it stayed.

Your worlds are different and
such they'll always remain.
She's dived back deep, probably to never be seen again!

Yet! You drool over the signs in the clouds that you see?
You know the land and the ocean aren't one,
they can't ever be!

With a smile on his face he pointed
at the shallow waters of the lake,
a look very carefully at the waves,
he was hinting them to make.

I may be a wanderer on land yet!
My heart now beats in the sea,
That! what is meant to be, always!
Finds its way back, you see!

Why Do I Still Dream About You?

Why do I still dream about you sometimes?
It's been a while that we've spoken for long in reality.
Yet dazing how I remember them dreams,
not in bits, but with complete clarity.

In ~~love~~ sync with poetry!

Why do I still dream about you sometimes?
When our chats have shrunk from paragraphs
and words to a few letters and emoticons?
When deep within our heartbeats tell us,
that we're not made for sprints but longer marathons.

Why do I still dream about you sometimes?

Is it coz you do think of me too
when you hear the chimes?
Or is it coz your brief catch up
after ages ended up in tiny rhymes?

I've waited for you since forever;
it almost feels like a lifetime.
Yet! Hoping there's a crescent moon you see on
the horizon, and you dream about me too sometime!

Kevin R Gandhi

The Lost Mermaid

Time passed, the mermaid was still lost at sea.
Hope however, is a miraculous virtue you see.

Move on, the world told him.
The explorer still felt lost.
This sudden mystery,
he felt compelled to solve at any cost.

In ~~love~~ sync with poetry!

He started frequenting the
exact spot where they met.
Hoping to catch a glance of her
in any way that he could get.

There had to be a reason that her eyes
and her smile in his dreams he could still see,
there had to be a reason he found peace
at this exact place where the land met the sea.

Years passed on, the legend remained about
an explorer that built a house in the middle of the sea,
about how he fell in love with a mermaid
and made her dreams his own destiny!

Same Boat Different Journeys

We could be sailing on the same boat,
yet! Be on different journeys.
We could be headed in the same direction,
yet! Our sails filled with different breeze.

Every sailor on this ship called "life"
has a specific role to play.
Some lost at sea for a long time,
some! Find their course right away.

The important part however!
Is, to enjoy this journey while it lasts.
Move "full ahead" with the wind of tomorrow
in our hopeful masts.

In love sync with poetry!

I Often Wonder

I often wonder what it would be like to witness
a sunrise from the peak of those mountains.
I often wonder what it would be like to cross
the frozen lakes and timid fountains.

I often wonder what it would be like
to be able to see all seven colors of the rainbow.
I often wonder where we'd be at,
if our words weren't cautiously flowing so slow.

I've often had visions and dreams
about meeting you in person;
have always believed that our paths crossed
at the right time for a reason.

I often wonder what it would be like
when we do finally meet.
The long ever-growing list
when we finally will get to complete.

Making Magic Happen

"I wana be there, I hope magic happens soon"
she wrote to him with half sleepy eyes.
A message this early in the morning
was surely a pleasant surprise.

"Amen! To that, Lemme see what I can do" he replied.
God only knew how much he prayed
for this day and how hard he had tried.

With a ticket in his hands, he left for
this magical place he had always heard about.
An enchanted forest of lights where reindeers
wandered in the night without doubt.

He travelled miles into the forest looking
for the man on a sleigh,
to get his help and figure out the fastest way.

To make magic happen one more time.
Just like the last one that "connected'
them over a rhyme!

In ~~love~~ sync with poetry!

Watch Your Dreams Come True

"You make the world seem so dreamy, how can I
possibly believe you?" she asked him with a doubt.
Confused about the applicable context, he asked
her what exactly it was about.

"The real world is fast" she replied,
"It brutally keeps flowing nonstop.
Gushes down desires and aspirations alike.
It's tough keeping them floating on the top.

"Agreed" he said smiling. "Take a look in that corner;
do you see how beautifully, the frozen waterfall
co-exists right next to the big one?"
That's exactly how you preserve your dreams
whilst always being on the run.

You choose that one special corner inside of your heart,
which remains at peace even
when rest of the world is falling apart.

"Believe" with all your heart,
it's all the universe expects from you.
"Believe" me with all your heart
and watch your dreams come true!

Is Love Enough?

Love! They say, happens when it has to happen.
Love! Changes your life in more
ways than you can imagine,

Yet! Is love enough?

Love! Has been the longest puzzling
mystery for humankind,
Love! Can stay out of sight for a long time
but never out of mind.

Yet! Is love enough?

Love! Is so easy to give and inversely tough to get.
The reality itself, it conveniently makes you forget.

Yet! Is love enough?

It's both! The disease and also the cure.
There's never been anything more
than love that's so pure!

Yet! Is love enough?

You can spend a lifetime pondering on the question
and that can surely take a while,
or just like me, you can let the rising heartbeats answer
or least take a hint from that smile!

In love sync with poetry!

The Road Unknown

Often in life you need to take the road unknown.
A path unexplored where no directions are shown.

A road that's surrounded with a haze of ambiguity.
A road that you'll probably end up
walking on till eternity.

The thing about the uncharted land.
Is that you can't keep expectations at hand.

Every sight you see on that road feels new,
every conversation like the first morning dew.

Don't be afraid, take a step forward and
trust them signs like that Divine light of ray.
Coz if it's meant to be, it will always find a way!

The Divine Light across the Sea

A small boat is all he had.
Yet! He chose to chase a divine light
he saw across the sea.
An entire ocean he'd have to cross,
in the unknown grey waters he knew he'll have to be.

What was it about this light
that he couldn't resist anymore?
Something deep within him seemed
to be yearning it from the core.

This mysterious light had kept
him enthralled for a long time.
Spellbound he was left trying
to decipher every rhyme.

Did he truly set out to find the light
or was this his journey of self-discovery
against his own might?

In ~~love~~ sync with poetry!

Crossing the coldest ocean on
the planet was not an easy task,
was he led by his heart or just accidental
mixed signals you may ask.

He knew he needed to "figure it out"
one single nautical mile every day.
"Did he make it?"
"Was it really worth it?"
Well! That's a story I will tell you another day.

Kevin R Gandhi

The City with Seven Islands

Mysterious, vibrant and attractive
this city looks from the outside.
To conquer and rule its basic heartbeats
for countless years many have always tried.

Kings, emperors and rulers this city had seen them all.
Never did history imagine
a wanderer figuring it out after all.

The wanderer! Different in his
ways that he looked at life.
Explored the off roads often with
a backpack and his lucky knife.

The very first sight of these seven islands
made him feel at home after a long time.
At peace he finally felt here, as if his destiny
was unfolding verse after verse within a rhyme.

Often lost he found himself
gazing into the eyes of the sky.
Time stood still, the full moon, the early rising sun,
everything just passing by.

Their story and his travelogue after that remains untold,
it is said within those seven islands
he found his own city of gold.

In ~~love~~ sync with poetry!

A Lot Like A Waterfall

"I told you already, I can't do this!"
she texted him out of nowhere.
"I tend to keep flowing. To remain stagnant
in the unknown is my biggest nightmare"

With a wise smile on his face he replied,
"I know you! You're just like a waterfall"
"Different from every other water body,
yet! Very basic and true to nature after all"

"I know that you've flowed through
very difficult terrains.
I got scars from my past too and
I know how much it pains"

"These rocks, they all look alike, yet!
Different minerals make them so unique from within.
Sometimes, you gotta have faith in the future,
forget the past and in your present, choose to begin."

"When it's meant to be, the right set of rocks will evolve
over time and around your flow they will cascade.
Creating a blissful lake, safe enough for you
to keep flowing along its side,
a forever that you no longer can evade!

A Cloudy Sky

"I don't know what I want" said the mermaid to the
sailor. "Everything usually ends up in a mess"
"Nothing so far has been usual you'd agree"
he tried assuring her.
Don't burden yourself with undesired stress.

"Besides, the thought of what could have been,
does that not perturb you in any way?"
"When you follow your heart laden with hope
there's always a light filled ray"

"Whilst I keep showing you the
brighter side of things" he continued,
"the sun seems to be setting on my horizon"
"I am known to be a wanderer without a cause
but this time I crossed oceans with a reason"

"I have circumnavigated the seven islands for a long
time now and I keep waiting longing to see a sign"
"If there's anything that I've learnt from the waves
in the sea is to fight for what's truly mine"

In ~~love~~ sync with poetry!

A blend of gold and blue like this in the sky,
the mermaid had never seen before.
Yet! Too scared she was to trust the signs,
too scared she was to leave the shore.

Thousands of miles of sailing,
yet! Did he make it across to her heart?
Or did the evils of their past and
the world forever kept them apart?
That's a story for another day,
I promise to begin from the very start.

A Sky Without Stars

A fortress around her; the princess had built.
In absence of a villain, she based it on a spurious guilt.

She spent most of her time within those walls,
only dreaming about blue lakes mountains and white waterfalls.

She no longer wished for a knight in shining armor.
Yet! A surreal connect she felt with this random wanderer.

With him she escaped on a few brief day trips.
Most of them accompanied with long conversations and chips.

She'd laugh; she'd giggle always with a sparkle in her eyes.
Momentarily! All dark clouds disappeared from her caged skies.

This was her first time breaking so many of her own set of rules.
After all, this felt real to her more than any affluent diamonds or jewels.

In ~~love~~ sync with poetry!

Yet! Unsure about how she'd manage
the unavoidable distance.
She steered the journey into the unknown,
again filled with turbulence.

"I can't think straight until I hear your heartbeats"
she told the wanderer.
Without blinking an eye, he took it off his chest
and handed it over to her.

"I cannot imagine a world without you, anymore"
he explained. "At least without the heart I think I'll
survive, I can try"
History remembers him as the wanderer,
who from that day, only had his moon
and no stars on his sky.

Can't Stop Won't Stop

Love! They say is usually sealed with a kiss.
Some don't get it right the first time, they probably miss.

Yet! Love is patient and love is persistent.
Being a bit slow in the process
Sometimes love is hesitant.

Love! They say is also very difficult to understand.
If you intend to at least walk on its path
come hold my hand.

Hold my hand on this road called life,
so we're able to explore it together.
I'd like getting lost with you by my side
as my prime navigator.

Holding hands, we'd keep driving to nowhere counting all signs.
Of a random song tuned in on the radio until it reminds.

In ~~love~~ sync with poetry!

Holding hands on the way make sure you keep
your hypnotizing eyes away from mine.
Coz every time in a gaze that they're locked,
I've had to pay a hefty fine.

Hold my hand until the rest we figure out together.
Hold my hand so you won't escape
like the sunny weather.

Hold my hand coz yours is a perfect fit with mine.
"I can't stop. I won't stop" Be it rain or shine!

The Wise Sorcerer

There's a legend about a mermaid,
a sailor and a wise sorcerer.
Whilst the other two were based at sea from ages,
the sailor was a recent foreigner.

The mermaid possessed magical healing
powers since centuries.
With which she had healed many sea creatures
of their unimaginable miseries.

However, consumed in this zany process
little did she realize?
She was slowly turning into stone,
not paying heed to anybody's advice.

To protect and cure her,
the sorcerer made every genuine attempt!
The mermaid with her charming ways however
always escaped in contempt.

In ~~love~~ sync with poetry!

"There has to be a way to bring her back. I'm ready to
risk my life" the worried sailor told the sorcerer.
"You don't have a clue of what you're
getting yourself into son "was his reply.
"You're merely a simple wanderer"

The sailor then persevered night and day treating
the mermaid with a magic potion one drop at a time.
They'd watch sunsets and sunrises together
talking to each other for hours coded in a rhyme.

Touched by their true affection for each other
the sorcerer built them a magical lighthouse by the sea.
Eliminating all the toxicities of yesterday,
their tomorrow forever was meant to be!

You're My Lobster

"Where have you been?" the worried wanderer
politely asked the mermaid.
"Be rest assured, I'm always fine" she snapped,
as any further questions she wanted to evade.

"I ransacked every pond but you, I still couldn't find"
"Concerned, I just was for anything
fishy running on your mind"

"I'm alright and I averse affection
from dear ones sometimes"
"Keep away from me temporarily coz
I'll be allergic to your advice and your altruistic rhymes"

"I grow these unsought claws sometimes and with them
I snap and clench with all my might"
"Get away while it's still safe,
let's avoid an unnecessary fight"

"I intend to build a bond" he explained "that remains
thick through the better and the worse"
"In sickness and in health like they say,
the entire rhyme and every verse"

"And about those claws I wouldn't
worry much little mermaid"
"You're my lobster!" that's what
Phoebe Buffay would've also said!

In ~~love~~ sync with poetry!

Old MonK & coKe
(15th May 2022)

This story is about how the coKe
and the old monk met.
As sometimes what you truly desire,
you indeed happen to get!

You see "coKe" was like no other ordinary drink.
She was bubbly, vivacious & full of energy to the brink.

The old monk wasn't as old as he sounded.
A lot of his qualities often left others astounded.

"coKe" usually only mixed with
things like ice that were clear.
For her, honesty and transparency
even if frozen were very dear.

The old monk sure seemed dark and doubtful
with his appearances.
Yet! For some reason she never could break away from
his soulful glances.

They liked each other's company
and were often found together.
He wished he had more time with
her coz then wasn't the perfect weather.

On a lazy Saturday afternoon,
they happened to get some time alone.
What they had kept suppressed,
exponentially within it had grown.

The last time he tried blending with her,
she hid behind a thin glass wall.
This time it went differently
coz it was meant to be after all.

To make sure she wanted it too,
he poured himself over her, in just a few little drops!
Their chemistry was instantaneous this time; they
blended passionately without any stops.

She sinked into his arms whilst their
eyes were lost deep into each other.
Never before did they blend so well to create
a magical drink this smoother.

In ~~love~~ sync with poetry!

She couldn't get enough of his caramelized after taste.
Him; on the other hand wanted things
a lot slower without any haste.

A few mixes done right,
she then demanded to be poured from the top.
He had completely surrendered himself;
he just wished she'd never stop.

Time wasn't on their side that day, inseparable they
wanted to be.
Yet! They had to give it away.
In their minds with closed eyes even today,
they wish forever in that moment they could stay!

Lakes with Our Names

"Talking in person by the lake works"
she texted him in a hurry.
Their stories with exchanged energies
she could no longer bury.

From that day onwards he was often found by a lake.
He'd travel long distances so a list of them
all he could make.

He wanted their first meeting
by the lake to be just as magical.
Even though few bits from her dream
were not completely practical.

He would spend hours at length staring
at clouds trying to find a concrete sign.
He'd visualize them lost in silent conversations, staring
at each other, sipping her favorite wine.

In ~~love~~ sync with poetry!

"I'm sure glad we got more lakes
than anyone else in the world"
he replied with a winking emoticon.
"We both have lakes on our name and to see
the remaining ones an entire decade we could be gone"

"Make it possible" she texted again,
sitting next to a window sipping a hot cup of tea.
Staring at the clouds hoping to spot a sign that
would assure her that it's truly meant to be!

Kevin R Gandhi

Living inside A Snowglobe

⋙✦⋘

In ~~love~~ sync with poetry!

Have you ever gazed into a snow globe
and imagined how living inside would feel for a while?
As I write about it, I cannot help but think about those
eyes and why they hide from me yet smile?

I cannot seem to get my eyes off you,
them being open or shut just doesn't matter.
The time we spent feels like a snow globe dream,
it kills me to see them shatter.

Never sail on two boats at the same time they said,
but I don't seem to have much of a choice.
It will find a way if it's meant to be,
until then be patient and persistent says my inner voice.

So here I am, on both the boats and on my knees,
I surrender to you oh! Universe,
with open arms I call out to you once again,
send me a sign, Please! Lift the curse!

Is It Ever A Goodbye?

Did you shed a tear for us when you saw me leave?
I even wore our names on my heart,
Coz in us I truly did believe!

To protect me from the dangers of the world
you gave me a fancy shield.
Compelled by your own futile laws
every emotion you concealed.

You tried hiding your honest eyes behind
the walls of your tiny hand.
But everything you wanted to say
was written on your headband.

"Don't stop! Won't stop" trust me
"I can't!" I have sincerely tried.
Trying to abide by your laws to my own heart,
I have miserably lied!

I'm sorry if I held you too tightly when I said
"I'll see you soon"
I didn't want to let you go coz I knew, I'd soon become
the wolverine and you "my moon".

In ~~love~~ sync with poetry!

It's been a thousand years already;
I still howl your name everyday looking at the sky.
But I ain't no kuekuatsheu, I will soon return to "your world" one last time to ask you "why"

Why did you shed a tear for "us"
when you saw me leave?
You can lie to yourself but "us"
you no longer can deceive.

My Sunrise V/S Your Sunset

If my hopeful sunrise could talk to
your clueless sunset in anyway.
It would mention how I keep waiting endlessly,
just to get a glimpse of you every day!

On my horizon you appeared like an enchanting
mermaid from a mysterious fairytale.
My attempts to get your undivided attention thereafter,
has been like the quest of the Holy Grail.

I know that you've dived back to the
deepest end of your life's cavernous ocean.
My heart still refuses to budge,
my eyes without blinking keep looking
for you with devotion.

Every day I come back with a hope filled heart,
to this shore where we had first met.
Despite the fact that centuries have passed,
your heartbeats these waves refuse to forget!

And until our worlds continue to witness
the sun setting and rising again, each day.
To bring you back forever this time
our destinies will conspire and find a way!

In ~~love~~ sync with poetry!

A Destiny – Manifested!

"Did you manifest all this?" she texted
him brimming with curiosity.
"Coz you've written about it in your poetries earlier and
a lot of it, as is, happened in reality"

"This is just the beginning!" he replied
with a playful smile.
"I've been conspiring night and day with the universe
for a while"

"Do you see us walking towards the sunset?"
he asked, sharing another picture he had clicked.
"Shush! No comments smarty" she replied with her
classic smirk, wanting to avoid being tricked.

"I've had a long and tiring day at work"
she texted again, now wanting to tease him a bit.
"So, I can't walk, you should've at least manifested a
comfy bench" she added, trying to test his grit.

"Lemme show u d bigger picture" he replied. "You see!
Destiny unfolds only at the right time"
He then sent her a zoomed-out version of his
manifestation, and the rest of it as a rhyme.

Sometimes! You'll need to zoom in too, to be able to see the dream I hold in my eyes.
And sometimes, you'll have to read the signs between them clouds on the heart of my skies.

And wait till you find out, about the manifestation list that I share every night with the moon.
Out of sight for some time, yet! Always on my mind you've been. I guess I'll just have to see you soon.

In ~~love~~ sync with poetry!

Into Your Eyes

I can't look into your eyes anymore.
I can't dive deeper; I'm safe by the shore.

I know you crossed oceans to meet me by the stream.
The rhymes we wrote together; seem like a half forgotten dream.

The intensity of your persistent imagination,
I can no longer bear.
It's easier to use an alibi and act as if I don't even care.

Yes! In reality I remember everything
like it was yesterday!
Yet! The more I try to find myself,
the more I end up feeling lost on the way.

And even though writing you off
might not be truly needed.
"I've managed" to win most my battles,
in my basic ways, I've always succeeded.

An exception you were, now you're
just collateral damage.
Nothing personal, I am evolving.
This is probably how I manage!

In love sync with poetry!

Away From Your Eyes

I can't look away from those eyes anymore!
For them! I'd traverse the seven seas all over again,
Scout every unknown seashore.

These thousand stones of your silence,
can't alter my flow of faith.
All seven colors of the rainbow unresponsive,
I have my hopes staked on the eighth.

I know that your eyes still dream with mine sometimes,
I know you still do imagine what it would be like,
living in our rhymes!

You trapped my soul when you
locked your eyes with mine.
Since then, you! It's just you
that they're trying to find.

So! You can look away all you like,
close your eyes, the reality, you refuse to see.
Deep within your heartbeats telling you
- he'll find way, Coz it's meant to be!

In ~~love~~ sync with poetry!

You may tear the pages of my stories
from the book of your life,
I ain't however, some words written with a chalk,
I am etched forever on the walls of your heart with a knife.

And no matter what chapter moving on
in your life you now try to read,
To the same rhymes your heart will beat again,
To this same spot every road you take; will lead.

www.ingramcontent.com/pod-product-compliance
Lightning Source LLC
LaVergne TN
LVHW061612070526
838199LV00078B/7253